ELOGIOS PARA *FLOCKS/REBAÑOS*

Una de las tantas voces de Fernando Pessoa preside y titula este poemario de Zurelys López-Amaya (*La Habana*, 1967). A diferencia de la diversidad propia de los heterónimos del ilustre portugués, rige aquí una voz única, identificable desde las primeras líneas hasta el último por su marca de género, por su rostro difuminado pero al mismo tiempo casi distinguible, que observa los puentes, los muros, los desplazamientos y las salidas en masa.

Algunas frases e imágenes, a manera de ritornelo, tanto en los poemas en prosa (estructura predominante del volumen) como en los versificados, reafirman la posibilidad de hallar en nosotros mismos la fuerza necesaria para vencer la inercia y encontrar "el camino correcto hacia el sol." Este último puede resumirse en el disfrute de ser libres y auténticos, así como en la plenitud amorosa de saber que alguien nos espera. Al término de cada uno de los sesenta textos, breves y sin arabescos formales que complejicen en exceso su lectura, esta nos incita a un silencio especial: el que se impone tras la honda reflexión de la buena poesía.

—Vitalina Alfonso, ensayista y editora, *La Habana*

PRAISE FOR *FLOCKS/REBAÑOS*

One of the many voices of Fernando Pessoa presides over and gives title to this collection of poems by Zurelys López-Amaya (*Havana*, 1967). In contrast with the diverse heteronyms of the illustrious Portuguese, one unique voice governs here, which is identifiable from the first lines to the last by virtue of its gendered nature, its blurred face that can just almost be made out, observing the bridges, the walls, the displacements, and the mass exoduses.

Some phrases and images, serving as chorus, not only in the prose poems (the predominant structure of the volume) but also in the poems in verse, reaffirm the possibility of finding in ourselves the strength necessary to vanquish our inertia and find "the right path toward the sun." This can be summed up as the pleasure of being free and authentic, just as in the loving plenitude of knowing that somebody awaits us. At the end of each one of the seventy texts, brief and without formal arabesques that overcomplicate their reading, this is what inspired in us a special silence: that which is inescapable after a deep reflection upon good poetry.

—Vitalina Alfonso, editor and critic, *Havana*

Con *Flocks/Rebaños* Zurleys López-Amaya enciende una cadena de hogueras que iluminan algunas de las más difíciles contradicciones y paradojas de la experiencia humana. Aquí somos "sombra" y "oquedad," y a la vez "luz" y "música;" estamos "solos y ciegos" y además "bienvenido[s] a la isla que hacemos minuciosamente;" y comprendemos que "la sangre de Caín está por doquier," pero también "el esplendor de la naturaleza porque esta existe." El toque del traductor, Jeffrey C. Barnett, es delicado y diestro, regalando a los lectores pleno acceso a los versos virtuosos de López-Amaya en una nueva lengua, exquisitamente chamuscada.

—Seth Michelson, Washington and Lee University

En este incitante libro, Zurelys López-Amaya examina con lúcida ternura la existencia colectiva del rebaño. Rodeado por lo no conocido, flanqueado por miedo, el rebaño sobrevive en una cuidadosa monotonía, pero no sin esperanza. Indiferente a los discursos políticos agobiantes, la libertad, *freedom,* es efímera pero constantemente posible. En *Flocks/Rebaños,* el lector experimenta la libertad como un objeto que apenas escapa nuestra visión—como la guagua que parece tardar años en llegar. La traducción al inglés está llena de afortunadas resoluciones. Aunque el libro ofrece una valiente comprensión de la realidad cubana; proporciona, además, algo para reflexionar a los lectores en todas partes.

—Pilar Cabrera Fonte, Augustana University

With *Flocks/Rebaños* Zurleys López-Amaya ignites a string of bonfires that illuminate some of the most difficult contradictions and paradoxes of human experience. Here we are "shadows" and "emptiness" while also being "light" and "music"; we are "alone and blind" while also "welcomed on the Island that we meticulously create;" and we understand how the "blood of Cain is everywhere," but so, too, is "the splendor of nature because it exists." The touch of the translator, Jeffrey C. Barnett, is as delicate as it is deft, gifting readers access to López-Amaya's virtuosic verse in an exquisitely scorched new tongue.

—Seth Michelson, Washington and Lee University

In this provocative book, Zurelys López-Amaya examines with lucid tenderness the collective existence of the flock. Encircled by the unknown, flanked by fear, the flock survives in cautious monotony but is not hopeless. Detached from tiresome political discourses, *la libertad*, freedom, is evasive yet constantly possible. In *Flocks/Rebaños* the reader experiences *la libertad* as an object just barely out of sight—like that bus taking forever to arrive. The English translation is full of felicitous resolutions. While the book is a courageous insight into Cuban reality, it will give pasture for thought to readers around the world.

—Pilar Cabrera Fonte, Augustana University

No es fácil encontrar un excelente poeta contemporáneo que de verdad te sobresalte, pero puedo aseverar que *Flocks/Rebaños* me ha afectado de esa forma. En *Flocks/Rebaños,* Zurelys López-Amaya magistralmente utiliza la dominante imagen del rebaño de ovejas para expresar preocupaciones filosóficas sobre la libertad, el instinto de rebaño de las masas, y el poder negativo de las consignas—y el control que estas ejercen sobre la gente. Pero lo que hace esta colección particularmente poética son las imágenes originales, y el impacto tantas veces chocante que tales imágenes producen en el lector. La traducción al inglés de estos poemas también es exitosa y creativa.

—Emilio Bejel, poeta, escritor e investigador,
University of California, Davis

Los prosoemas bilingües de *Flocks/Rebaños,* de la poeta cubana Zurelys López-Amaya, tan bellamente traducidos al inglés por Jeffrey C. Barnett, dramatizan vívidamente una variedad de emociones, desde la desesperanza a la celebración de la sobrevivencia (aunque hay que pagar el precio). Los poemas examinan el frecuentemente siniestro poder de las identidades colectivas (el rebaño) que una sociedad compartida nos impone a todos, y los miedos y limitaciones que pesan sobre cada ser humano.

—Mary G. Berg, Brandeis University

It is not easy to find an excellent contemporary poet that really startles you, but I can say that *Flocks/Rebaños* has had that effect on me. Zurelys López-Amaya in *Flocks/Rebaños* masterfully uses the dominant image of the sheep flocks to express philosophical concerns about liberty, sheepish behavior of the masses, and the negative power of the control exercised by slogans. But what makes this collection particularly poetic is the original images, and the often shocking impact that those images produce in the reader. The English translation of the poems is also very successful and creative.

—Emilio Bejel, poet, writer and scholar,
University of California, Davis

The bilingual prose poems of *Flocks/Rebaños*, by the Cuban poet Zurelys López-Amaya, beautifully translated into English by Jeffrey C. Barnett, vividly dramatize emotions ranging from despair to celebration of survival (albeit at a price). The poems examine the often sinister power of collective identities (the flock) that a shared society imposes upon us all and the fears and limitations that burden all living beings.

—Mary G. Berg, Brandeis University

Los bellos prosoemas de Zurelys López-Amaya narran con una voz a la vez individual y colectiva, política y surreal. El engañosamente lúcido estilo renueva un imaginario cubano familiar y un lenguaje simbólico universal, lo cual le da una apremiante resonancia a la colección. Las traducciones bien pensadas de Jeffrey Barnett dejan que el lector comprenda los poemas en diálogo y en coro con la totalidad de ellos—que los acerque no individualmente, sino como rebaño.

—Janet Hendrickson, translator

Esta edición bilingüe de *Flocks/Rebaños* permite al lector angloparlante entrar en en el abigarrado mundo literario de la poeta cubana Zurelys López-Amaya. El volumen abre con fragmentos de prosa en que en que se oye reflexionar a una oveja sobre la existencia cotidiana de la manada. Un pícaro ejercicio en alegoría, se sigue por textos que hacen hincapié en los objetos y actividades de todos los días. La colección resalta la destreza que tiene López-Amaya tanto con el verso blanco como con la prosa en miniatura, mientras Jeffrey C. Barnett logra la difícil hazaña de traducir un lenguaje tan engañosamente simple. Este volumen, editado por Nancy Alonso y Katherine Hedeen, claramente es un acto de amor y una maravillosa adición a la creciente obra de literatura cubana en traducción al inglés.

—Naomi Lindstrom, University of Texas at Austin

Zurelys López-Amaya's beautiful *prosoemas* speak in a voice that is at once individual and collective, political and surreal. Their deceptively lucid style renovates a familiar Cuban imaginary and a universal symbolic language to lend the collection a resonant urgency. Jeffrey Barnett's considered translations allow the reader to understand these poems in conversation and in chorus with each other—to approach them not just individually, but, as it were, to join their flock.

—Janet Hendrickson, translator

This bilingual edition of *Flocks/Rebaños* allows English-language readers to enter the variegated literary world of the Cuban poet Zurelys López-Amaya. The volume opens with fragments of prose in which a sheep is overheard ruminating on the quotidian existence of herd animals. This sly exercise in allegory is followed by texts that focus attention on everyday items and activities in and of themselves. The collection showcases López-Amaya's dexterity in both free verse and prose miniatures, while Jeffrey C. Barnett manages the difficult feat of translating misleadingly simple language. This volume, edited by Nancy Alonso and Katherine Hedeen, is clearly a labor of love and a wonderful addition to the growing body of Cuban literature in English translation.

—Naomi Lindstrom, University of Texas at Austin

FLOCKS

REBAÑOS

FLOCKS

—REBAÑOS—

ZURELYS LÓPEZ AMAYA
TRANSLATED BY JEFFREY C. BARNETT

Cubanabooks

Published in the United States of America by Cubanabooks.

400 W. 1st St., Dept. ILLC, California State University, Chico

Chico, California 95929-0825

Printed in the United States of America

Cover design: Kellen Livingston

Cover Photos: Sara E. Cooper

Text design: Kellen Livingston

Cubanabooks logo art: Krista Yamashita

English language editor: Katherine M. Hedeen

Spanish language editor: Nancy Alonso

Editor in Chief: Sara E. Cooper

First Edition

10 9 8 7 6 5 4 3 2 1

Library of Congress Control Number: 2016948998

ISBN: 978-1-944176-08-2

ÍNDICE / CONTENTS

SOBRE *REBAÑOS*
POR DANIEL DÍAZ MANTILLA

Ser rebaño es abdicar de sí, de la libertad individual, de los rasgos y criterios personales, para fundirse en una masa moldeable, manipulable. Ser rebaño es la apoteosis y también la caricatura de lo colectivo, es dejarse conducir por intereses que no son los propios, rendir las diferencias ante la presión de una unidad absoluta, tiránica. Quien ha vivido en el rebaño conoce de primera mano la experiencia de disolverse, de anularse, de ser tenido como un número.

Este libro nos coloca, desde el título hasta el último de sus versos, ante este tipo de experiencias. El desamparo, la resistencia y la angustia de una persona ante la masa; el contacto cotidiano con los límites, el control y las presiones sociales, dan a esta voz su fuerza y su autenticidad.

Pastoreado en el absurdo, conminado a una mansedumbre total, el individuo se resiste, testimonia en soledad —acaso para nadie— el asedio mudo del rebaño, su aparente unanimidad, la inercia de cumplir solícitos o temerosos una incuestionable voz de mando que los guía en círculos, del redil, al forraje, al matadero. Es precisamente ese testimonio, desafío sereno pero firme al silencio, a la violencia cotidiana, el contenido de este libro: huella del malestar y la esperanza, semilla del individuo en el rebaño, poesía al margen del control, como toda verdadera poesía.

ABOUT *FLOCKS*
BY DANIEL DÍAZ MANTILLA

To be a flock is to abdicate one's selfhood, one's individual liberty, one's personal traits and principles, in order to sink into a malleable mass open to manipulation. To be a flock is both the exaltation and caricature of the collective; that is to say, it means allowing oneself to be driven by goals that are not one's own, surrender differences under the pressure of an absolute, tyrannical unity. Whoever has lived in a flock knows firsthand the experience of dissolving oneself, of destroying oneself, of allowing oneself to become nothing but a number.

This book, from its title to its final lines, places us among such experiences. Helplessness, resistance, and the anguish of a person confronted by the masses; daily exposure to limits, control, and social pressure; these facets forge the strength and authenticity of the poetic voice.

Being herded into absurdity, coerced into total docility, the individual fights back, giving lonely testimony—perhaps to no one—of the flock's mute siege, its apparent unanimity, its obsequious or fearful obedience to an indisputable voice leading them in circles, from their pen, to the pasture, to the slaughterhouse. This book consists of just such a testimony, one that serenely yet firmly defies the flock's silence, its daily violence. Here we find traces of unease and hope, the seed of the individual existing within the flock, poetry existing at the margins of control, as does all true poetry.

TRANSLATOR'S NOTE
BY JEFFREY C. BARNETT

In contemporary Cuban literature, women writers of fiction and poetry continue to offer exciting and unique works that challenge preconceived notions of a setting that is rapidly changing. Among others for example, the texts of Nancy Morejón, Mirta Yáñez, Uva de Aragón, Nancy Alonso, and Georgina Herrera speak to a deep and personal relationship with the Island's present and past. Zurelys López Amaya joins the corpus of Cuban women writers as one of the most recent voices to receive national and international attention. In a short time, she has produced a sizeable contribution to Cuban letters, including *Pactos con la sombra* (2009) *[Pacts with the Shadows]*, *Rebaños* (2010) *[Flocks]*, *Minúsculos espejos* (2011) *[Tiny Mirrors]*, *La señora solitaria* (2013) *[The Solitary Lady]*, *Lanzar la piedra* (2015) *[To Throw the Stone]*, and *Levitaciones* (2015) *[Levitations]*. The volume presented here, *Rebaños / Flocks*, constitutes the first full-length translation of one of her works into English. Recognized for its refreshing and unusual style—or as one critic has described it, "overwhelming and sincere"—*Flocks* includes some poetic selections that may seem polemical, and yet readers also may find the poems serene and detached.

Although López Amaya occasionally employs traditional free verse poems, the most prevalent form throughout the volume is that of the "prose poem." In "We Were Flocks," the *prosoema* allows her sufficient space to develop the traditional allegory of the pastor and his flock, thus the title of the work. Infused with an aesthetically poetic tone, the vision and imagery of the extended metaphor lead the reader to consider disturbing questions about modern-day Cuba. In a convincing and lyrical manner, she portrays a society amassed in a pasture hopelessly waiting for an absent shepherd. In conventional pastoral literature, Western poetry has focused typically on the shepherd. In this case, however, the poet leads our eye back to the flock, or rather the Cuban people. In doing so, she puts forth a complex and ambivalent view, one that is an instinctual lament and also one that finds solace in poetry.

Despite the work's poignant socio-political insight, López Amaya's poetry does not rest solely on a social thesis. Instead, she offers a rich and complex view of her world. For example, in the second part—"The Reflection of the Walls"—she moves away from the macro level of society and focuses on seemingly mundane concerns. In the tradition of Pablo Neruda's *Odes,* she contemplates her immediate surroundings in an effort to reveal an object's overlooked significance. Quotidian matters—such as her garden, a dog, or a desk chair—and everyday people—such as fishermen at the dock, the man who sharpens knives, or a street performer—capture her poetic eye, and that in turn attempts to convince us that no thing is truly commonplace. Her reflections are not limited to the tangible, however. She profoundly expresses pathos by confronting and accepting nostalgia, remorse, longing, and love. Her poems project a wide array of emotion, including empathy for a Holocaust survivor ("Naked"), wistfulness upon going back to her hometown ("There's A Town..."), the loneliness of an empty street ("The Avenue"), and aesthetic wonder as she describes the mansion where she works and where the poet Dulce María Loynaz lived ("...pure solitude is mine alone"). In short, whether posing disturbing images about her socio-political milieu or celebrating the mundane, *Flocks* provides the reader with a gestalt of the poet's daily life, a vision that on the one hand is inextricably tied to Cuba, while on the other, it extends beyond the island to summon the universal.

RECREATING A POETIC WORK

The translator frequently faces difficult choices when trying to render literature into a new original. Poetry by its nature should be ambiguous, and translations should avoid being interpretations. Succinctly, translation is about choices. Does a word convey too many things? Does it mean the same thing in different contexts? Does it sound right? What makes a word a better choice? There are some good reasons why editors, readers, translators, and, of course, the original author disagree at times on the word selection. Translators of poetry have to consider expressiveness, tone, double entendres, resonance, and cultural innuendo, among other obstacles. The challenge, then, is to select a word that still maintains the same ambiguity, avoids jumping to the symbolic meaning, and moves beyond a transliteration.

López Amaya's style is characteristically straightforward and direct, which surprisingly can create problems in finding a suitable equivalent in English. For example, without much argument the word *desnudo* would suggest the translation "naked." Nonetheless, what seems to be an uncomplicated conversion can be misleading when one considers its wide range of possible images: nude, bare, in one's birthday suit, to be decent, and so on. Moreover, knowing that the reader may jump to the conclusion of the word's suggestive or erotic meaning, López Amaya catches us by surprise when she employs it to convey the helplessness of an Auschwitz prisoner, or the freedom she feels strolling through her hometown, or the vulnerability when facing one's surroundings. The ambivalence in the Spanish word *libertad* provides another example. Unquestionably *libertad* denotes "liberty" in Spanish, but it's also the same word for "freedom." While at first both words seem to be equivalents, philosophers will argue that there is a significant difference between the lack of restraint imposed by an authority (or liberty) and the individual power to act (or freedom). In such cases, the poet in Spanish can employ a single word that conjures up multiple notions, but the translator has to wade through the possibilities and hopefully choose correctly.

In addition to word selection, a translator must also consider tone and sound. In several poems López Amaya refers to *aves*, which simply means "birds." Arguably, however, the open phonemic sound of *aves* carries with it a poetic quality that isn't conveyed in the English word "birds" and certainly not in "fowl." The same is true for the melodic quality of *mordida*, "bite." "Chomp" sounds too ugly, "gnaw" too nasal, "nibble" too delicate. One can often find ways of working around such challenges, but sometimes the solution leads us to rely on a descriptive phrase. For example, the Spanish word *caminante* literally means "walker" but my ear perceives that it has a certain gait to it. In Antonio Machado's *"Caminante, no hay camino"* for example, the reader can hear the beat and the rhythm of someone walking. The transliteration however—"Walker, there isn't a path"— sounds more like someone stumbling along. When López Amaya employed the same cadence, I couldn't bring myself to say "walker," and certainly not the recreational "hiker" or overbearing "sojourner." Instead, I opted for an adjectival clause: "the path will once again become useful for the one *walking*."

Sounds are not limited to the phonemic quality within a single word. When one strings them together, they produce a tone. In "Coming Back," for example, I imagine a soft-spoken narrator who is barely audible: "I come back to your bare skin…." Akin to Neruda's "I Like It When You're Still," the tone is more of a whisper. By contrast, other poems such as "Nightfall" bring to mind a biblical tone reminiscent of the Psalms: "Lead us not into temptation and free us, O Lord, when clarity overshadows us."

In addition to word selection and tone imitation, translators have to consider how much of the story to reveal. Most readers would rightfully guess that Ernesto refers to Che Guevara, but there are less obvious references that tempted me to add a note or explain too much in the text. For example, in the poem framed in López Amaya's hometown of San Antonio de los Baños ("There Is a Town…"), she longingly remembers Quidiello, Silvio, Abela, and "El Loco." Quidiello, or Rubén Suárez Quidiello, is known for his paintings of landscapes, in this case along the Ariguanabo River. Silvio refers to Silvio Rodríguez, one of the co-founders of the *Nueva Trova* style of music, and Abela and "El Loco" refer to Cuban caricaturists Eduardo Abela (1889–1965) and René de la Nuez (1938–2015), both local artists known for their biting political humor. Other poems include a dedication or make subtle allusions that might require context, but in the age of electronic information, I opted to leave the reader to her own devices and to receive the poem as it was in its original, without commentary or explanation.

In summary, whether choosing a word based on its sound, the tone it conveys, or its transliterated directness, as translators we consider a host of options before settling on one sole word. Perhaps later we wish we had gone with a different choice, but I imagine the translation process of vacillation and regret is not too different than in the original process when the poet herself contemplates word selection. In the end, however, both the poet and translator would accept that the more important creative act is the one carried out by the reader, who ultimately decides the significance assigned to the words and the images they bring to mind.

ACKNOWLEDGEMENTS

I remember very well that day in Panama when Sara E. Cooper sent me an electronic copy of *Rebaños*. To Sara, I'm grateful to you for introducing me to the rich poetry that López Amaya has produced and will continue to offer. To Zurelys and Daniel, I am indebted to you for your help in working through difficult passages, both during our various meetings in Havana and later through our many emails. Thank you so much for your friendship and encouragement. To our editors, Kate Hedeen and Nancy Alonso, thank you for your keen eyes and professional skill. To my colleagues and students at Washington and Lee University, I am always appreciative of your advice and support. I am especially grateful to Cindy Rivas, who worked closely with me on a number of poems. And finally, as with all things in life, I wouldn't want to complete any milestone without sharing it with Kathleen and my wonderful daughters, Whitney and Jessie. Everything I do is always dependent upon your gracious patience and support.

A mi hija Lisandra,

A mi madre y familia,

A Verónica Aranda,

A Ena Lucía Portela,

A Edmundo Desnoes,

A Yeney y Raúl Flores,

A Rafael Alcides por aquellos tiempos,

A Daniel por existir,

A Salvador Ferrer, en su memoria.

To my daughter Lisandra,

To my mother and family,

To Verónica Aranda,

To Ena Lucía Portela,

To Edmundo Desnoes,

To Yeney and Raúl Flores,

To Rafael Alcides for those times,

To Daniel for existing,

To Salvador Ferrer, in his memory.

REBAÑOS

Comprendí que las cosas son reales y todas tan diferentes las unas de las otras;
lo comprendí con los ojos, nunca con el pensamiento.
Comprender esto con el pensamiento sería hallarlas todas iguales.

Fernando Pessoa
(bajo el heterónimo Alberto Caeiro)
"Si después de mi muerte..."

FLOCKS

I understood that things are all real and different one from the other.
I understood this with my eyes, never with my thoughts.
To understand this with one's thoughts would make them seem all the same.

Fernando Pessoa
(under the heteronym Alberto Caeiro)
"If After My Death..."

FUIMOS REBAÑOS

1.

Fuimos los rebaños del día. Tropezamos a diario con piedras que emergen de los ríos y esperamos callados el sonido de una flauta que hace retornar al rebaño. Comemos lo mismo todos los días. Hierba verde y seca por momentos. Miramos al sol ponerse en el mismo amanecer. Apenas pensamos en lo que dejamos atrás mientras el tiempo no se detuvo, ni acampó para esperar por nuestro retorno hacia el camino, hacia la misma granja, la misma noche de ovejas durmiendo para comenzar el día amontonados y callados en la colina que da al otro lado del barranco. Somos quietas ovejas que prefieren el equilibrio del lugar, la hierba alta donde apenas se nota nuestra presencia. El silbido de una flauta nos conduce siempre al mismo sitio que queda al otro lado del barranco.

WE WERE FLOCKS

1.

We were the flocks of the day. Daily we stagger over the rocks that protrude from the rivers, and silently we wait for the sound of the flute that calls back its flock. We graze on the same thing each day. Grass, green and, at times, brown. We watch the sun set just as we see it rise. We seldom think about what we have left behind since time has never stopped or lingered long enough to wait for us to head back to the path, back to the same farmyard, back to the same night of sheep sleeping so they can begin tomorrow huddled and silent on the hill that faces the other side of the ravine. We are peaceful little lambs who prefer to maintain the balance of the place, who prefer the high grass where we are barely visible. The flute's whistle leads us ever back to the very same site on the other side of the ravine.

2.

Somos rebaños. Nadie desvela por proteger nuestra lana, nadie nos prepara el camino hacia el polvo que cubrirá nuestro cuerpo. La noche será nuestra, será el descanso y la seguridad de saber que mañana es un día igual a otro. Tendremos los mismos gustos. Caminaremos por el mismo sendero cubierto de hierbas verdes y secas por momentos. Veremos los rostros acomodados contra el aire, comprimidos y exánimes de tanto andar, dura la piel por el sol. En la colina vemos a un hombre arrodillado que implora la oquedad de los días, la forma de redimir culpas por no encontrar el camino correcto hacia el sol.

2.

We are flocks. No one bothers to protect our wool. No one tends the path that will cover our hides in dust. Ours will be the night. It will be our rest and haven, our assurance that tomorrow will be like any other day. We will have the same yearnings. We will roam the same path covered in green and, at times, brown grass. We will see our faces, fixed against the wind, taut and lifeless from so much walking, skin withered from the sun. On the hill we see a man kneeling, imploring the emptiness of our days, begging for a way to be absolved for not having found the right path towards the sun.

3.

Los rebaños no se quejan de la lluvia en sus cuerpos
ni de las veces que tienen que escuchar el silbido del
hombre sobre sus cabezas. No se quejan mientras el olor
a hierba húmeda trafica con el viento hacia otras colinas.
¡Avisad a los otros que esperan callados el sonido de
una flauta! El hombre que implora ha envejecido con
sus preguntas y ha decidido entrar al rebaño.

3.

Flocks don't complain about the rain that falls on their fleece or about the number of times they have to hear the call of the flute that hovers above their heads. They don't complain as long as the smell of the moist pasture travels in the wind to the neighboring hills. Send the word to all who await silently the call of the flute! The man who kneels has become old with his questions and has decided merely to join the flock.

4.

Allá afuera donde el rebaño sigue siendo generoso,
complaciente en su quietud a pesar de no ver otra
cosa que hierba verde y seca por momentos, fluyen
los álamos y otras ciudades con sus luces, otros ríos
que llevan y traen mensajes incitándonos a fluir con
ellos. Mientras el rebaño toma la forma de las colinas
y mantiene el ritmo de ser conforme con su quietud,
aparecen señales que indican la manera de no huir en
busca del tiempo. El tiempo es el destino de la soledad
hacia lo que luego nos parece infinito.

4.

Out there the flock is still generous, complacent in
its stillness, despite not seeing anything other than
green, or at times brown, grass in the pasture. Out
there cottonwood trees and other cities with lights
abound. Other rivers bring messages back and forth
tempting us to converge with them. As the flock takes
on the form of the surrounding hillsides and persists
in its equanimity, signs emerge that show us how to
avoid going off in search of time. Time is solitude's
destination toward what seems infinite.

5.

Uno intenta subir a la cima. La duda lo confina, lo induce a no seguir, a quedarse con los demás que muestran sabiduría en la quietud, en el silencio. Alguien exporta lana de mis ovejas. De mí. Del que intenta subir a la cima que de pronto parece la nada. Y es la nada eso que nos rodea, eso que nos envuelve en cada minuto retorcido. La nada inmensa que rompe en los arrecifes de cualquier isla: el agua como un fenómeno circunstancial. En todas las islas hay una barca esperando. Barca que rompe en los arrecifes. Yo no intento subir a la cima. Dudo entre la noche y mis sueños.

5.

One tries to climb to the top, but doubt holds one back. It tempts one not to go any further, to stay back with the others who show wisdom in their stillness, in their silence. Someone is exporting the wool from my sheep. From me. From the one who tries to climb to the top, the top which suddenly seems like nothingness. And it is nothingness that surrounds us, that envelops us every twisted moment. A vast nothingness that breaks upon the reefs of every island: water being a circumstantial phenomenon. At every island there is always a boat that waits. Boats that break upon the reefs. I don't try to climb to the top. I waver between the night and my dreams.

6.

Traslado mi espanto hacia el cuarto que corrige mis instintos. Me dejo llevar por el hombre que navega conmigo dentro de la manada y lloramos juntos, amamos juntos el placer de sentir el aire desde las colinas y seguimos.

6.

I shift my fear back to the room that puts in check
my instincts. I let myself be carried along by the man
who wanders with me in the flock and we cry together,
together we love the pleasure of feeling the air from
the hills and we continue on.

7.

La cima no es lo que nos permite ver desde el ojo. Son nuestros huesos andantes y algo del pensamiento que corrige dudas. La piedra está en el camino, la tomamos para guardarla y decir que es nuestra. Pero no es nuestra la piedra, es del camino. Cruzamos en busca de respuestas. Es del rebaño en la colina la piedra. Si fuésemos la colina miraríamos con tristeza al rebaño. Todos los días lo mismo, amontonados en su quietud pensante, callados como mudas ovejas, conformes con su hierba verde y por momentos seca en el prado, al pie de la colina. Cuando se sube a una colina a mirar, podemos ver los muros que simulan nubes. Alguien cree que cruzar el cielo significa alguna cosa. Desde las colinas sentimos el placer del aire en nuestro rostro.

7.

It is not the summit that allows our eyes to see. It is
our rambling bones and a bit of thinking that corrects
our doubts. A rock is on the path, and we pick it up
and claim it. But the rock does not belong to us. It
belongs to the path. We cross the road in search of
answers. The rock belongs to the flock on the hill. If
we were the hill we would look upon the flock with
sadness. Every day the same thing, huddled together
in their thoughtful stillness, silent like muted sheep,
content with their green, or at times brown, grass in
the pasture at the foot of the hill. When we climb
a hill to look about, we see walls that look like
clouds. Someone thinks that crossing the sky means
something special. From the top of the hill we feel
the pleasure of the wind in our face.

8.

Hay un dios en mi barca que antes no veía. Me dice
que la cima es buen camino. Que guarde la piedra del
camino para enseñar a los viajeros de mi barca la luz que
existe fuera de las colinas. El placer del aire que golpea
nuestro rostro es casi exánime, estridente en el pasto
que defeco cada día. Ser el pasto es la oportunidad de
igualarme a quienes creen que no podemos vivir con
el mismo alimento por décadas. Fuera de las colinas
existe una luz. Todos somos el pasto.

8.

There is a god on my boat I hadn't noticed before. He tells me the top is a good path, that I should pick up a rock and show it to those who travel with me in my boat as proof that light exists beyond the hills. The pleasant air that strokes our faces is almost lifeless; harshly it blows in the pastures where I empty my bowels each and every day. Being the pasture means the opportunity to become one with those who think we cannot survive on the same food for decades. Beyond the hills a light exists. All of us are the pasture.

9.

Algo permea la sonrisa en mis labios de oveja. Miro
la cuerda de los hombres en mi pensamiento y salgo
a la calle a recordar que somos ovejas en una colina,
que miramos calladas el otro lado del barranco sin
ver, sin cruzar hacia lo desconocido por temor de no
regresar a nuestro sitio de siempre, donde todas las
miradas se parecen.

9.

Something seeps through my smiling sheep lips. In my thoughts I see the actions of men and I go out into the street so I can remember we are still sheep on a hill, that silently we look at the other side of the ravine without seeing, without crossing into the unknown for fear of not coming back to our usual place, where everyone resembles each other.

10.

Soy el pasto. Soy las ovejas y mis colinas. Ya no somos
rebaño porque somos parte del rebaño que se es para
no seguir conformes. Ser una cosa u otra es lo mismo
que ser en medio de tanto no haber sido. Mientras
somos nos alimentamos de consignas. Hasta llegamos
a creer en ellas de tanto que somos parte del rebaño
que se es. Y no aprendo de las consignas. La estampa
de algún viajero se quedó en el camino. Aprendo
del rebaño que no somos sin el silbido de una flauta
que alguien toca para apagar su pena de no ser más
que el hombre debajo del árbol en la colina. Somos
raras ovejas que escuchan amontonadas por temor a
los perros que ignoran la bondad de ovejas temerosas.
Subiremos una a una hasta la cima, silenciosas como
los mangles de la India, oiremos la flauta del ovejero
acicalar nuestras mentes, pero ninguna querrá oír las
mismas notas musicales para regresar a la granja. Será
un día azul y cada oveja querrá un nombre diferente,
un olor diferente entre tantos olores que confunden.

10.

I am the pasture. I am the sheep and my hills. We are not a flock any longer because we became part of the flock that chose not to be contented. To be one thing or the other is the same thing as being in the middle of never having been. While we exist we feed on slogans. We even come to believe in them so much we become rooted in the flock that exists. And I don't learn from slogans. The image of some traveler was left on the path. I have learned from the flock that we do not exist without the sound of the flute that someone plays to ease the pain of being nothing more than the man under a tree on the hill. We are unusual sheep that listen huddled together out of fear from the dogs that do not recognize the goodness of frightened sheep. We shall reach the summit one by one, serenely like mangroves from India. We will hear the pastor's flute attempt to bedeck our minds, but no one will wish to hear the same musical notes calling them back to the homestead. It will be an azure day, and each sheep will want its own name, its own smell among so many smells that mingle.

EL PARADERO

1.

La libertad es una figura abstracta entre círculos de distantes cosas rotas. Las cosas rotas figuran una calle igual a un paradero, donde los que esperan la libertad de ser personas otra vez tampoco esperan que llegue el ómnibus a tiempo.

THE BUS STOP

1.

Freedom is an abstract figure among circles of distant broken objects, among which a street amounts to as much as a bus stop, where those who long for freedom to be people once again hopelessly wait for the bus to arrive on time.

2.

La libertad de este cuerpo que no aprende a mudar es indisoluble, demora en el ocaso de la espera. La melodía se bifurca en el traspaso de la melodía. Hace que el ave retorne al ómnibus y sea paciente con su tiempo. Nos obliga a ser conscientes en la espera.

2.

The freedom of this body that refuses to bend is unbreakable. It drags its feet in the twilight of waiting. The melody splits in two as it goes along. It leads the birds to take the bus again and bide their time patiently. It obliges us to be aware while we wait.

3.

La libertad revolotea en las manos del que limpia
las calles y recorre las avenidas como fantasma o
mariposa. Qué más da. La espera de algo sobre el
techo nos sostiene en su lentitud.

3.

Freedom flutters in the street sweeper's hands as it floats through the streets like a ghost or butterfly. What difference does it make? The expectation of something atop the roof holds us with its slowness.

4.

La libertad desaparece a la par del agua que corre
distraída por los muros. El agua que corre resulta
fina y transparente. Solo es agua en los muros, luego
desaparece ante el tiempo y la esfinge. Desaparece en
torno a la crueldad de sostenernos sobre el agua que
cae, que corre distraída por los muros.

4.

Freedom disappears along with the water that ambles distractedly over the walls. The trickling water emerges pure and transparent. It is only water while on the walls; later it disappears in the presence of time and the sphinx. It disappears due to the cruelty of keeping us afloat above the water that falls, that ambles distractedly along the walls.

5.

La libertad se esconde. Nos sostiene la esfera imaginaria que responde a los instintos del paradero, aquí donde los autobuses reflejan el tiempo que nos atrapa en telarañas, como una mentira. También nos trae la calma. Debemos permanecer callados mientras los animales del circo viajan y llenan su carpa en otras capitales. Viajan y juegan los animales de circo.

5.

Freedom shrouds itself. The imaginary sphere that responds to the instincts of the Bus Stop sustains us, here where the buses mirror time that traps us in spider webs, like a lie. It also soothes us. We must remain silent while the circus animals travel and fill their tents in other cities. The circus animals travel and frolic.

6.

La libertad nos busca entre las balsas mutiladas, en el cometa de un niño que mira al cielo y vuela con el cielo, y ama y vuelve a volar como si fuese él ese cometa que lanza su cuerpo contra el aire.

6.

Freedom searches for us among the mangled rafts, upon the kite of a child who looks to the sky and who flies into the heavens, and loves, and soars time and again as if he were the very kite throwing his body against the air.

7.

La libertad no es la nada que huye por no alcanzarte,
ni la familia que llega de otras capitales con regalos
para aliviar la pena. Los regalos alivian la pena del
que cruza la misma calle, el mismo banco con sus aves
sin color mirando hacia la nada.

7.

Freedom is not that emptiness that takes flight
whenever it can't reach you, and it's not family
members who come from other cities with gifts to
ease the pain. Gifts ease the pain for those who cross
the same street, the same bench with its colorless
birds gazing off into the emptiness.

8.

La libertad no es esto que deprime, no es el tiempo que padecemos. No es tiempo la libertad, no es el muro ni el agua que cae sobre la hierba que nos alimenta los ojos. La libertad no es la palabra dicha, ni la figura abstracta entre círculos de distantes cosas rotas. La libertad es el aire que golpea nuestro rostro cada vez que salimos a ver lo que no se tiene.

8.

Freedom is not something that disheartens, nor the hours we endure. Freedom is not time, not the wall, not the water that falls upon the grass that feeds our eyes. Freedom is not the spoken word or an abstract figure among circles of distant broken objects. Freedom is the air that slaps us in the face each time we venture out to see what we are lacking.

EL JARDÍN

1.

Siembro un jardín cada día. Miro crecer el jardín con triste placer de no saber si la tierra soportará el amor con que siembro. La tierra es seca y llena de piedras que buscan hacer un camino. Recojo las piedras para ver crecer nuestro jardín. Quito las orugas de mi rosa y salgo cansada del intento. No es el tiempo que pasa mientras se hace un jardín, es el dolor de la rosa con orugas.

THE GARDEN

1.

I tend a garden each day. I watch the garden grow with a sad pleasure of not knowing if the ground will be able to bear the love with which I tend it. The soil is dry and full of rocks that are trying to make a path. I gather the rocks in order to watch our garden grow. I remove the caterpillars from my roses and I wind up exhausted from my efforts. It is not the time spent in creating a garden. It is the pain of dealing with the rose's caterpillars.

2.

Siembro un jardín cada día. Sé que no hallaremos el lado opuesto de las migajas, ni el porqué de mis manos que insisten en limpiar la tierra de sus piedras. Una piedra es la muestra del camino que volverá a ser útil para el caminante. Una piedra es el camino.

2.

I tend a garden each day. I know we will never find
the other side of the dirt or the answer to why my
hands insist on culling the rocks from the land. A
rock is proof that the path will once again become
useful for the one walking. A rock is the path.

3.

Siembro un jardín cada día. Cada semilla traerá el
placer de verlo crecer sin mentiras. No será mi jardín
el poder de una cosa sobre otra. Será bienvenido a la
isla que hacemos minuciosamente dentro de esta casa.
Mi isla es este jardín inmenso que crece sin mentiras,
sin intercambio de monedas. Miro crecer el jardín
con triste placer. No sé si la tierra soportará el amor
con que siembro. Siembro un jardín cada día. Será un
bosque este jardín.

3.

I tend a garden each day. Each seed will bring the pleasure of watching it grow without lies. My garden will not be the power of one thing over another. All will be welcomed on the Island that we meticulously create within this house. My Island is this immense garden that grows without lies, without the exchange of money. I watch the garden grow with a sad pleasure. I don't know if the ground will be able to bear the love with which I tend it. I tend a garden each day. This garden will be a forest.

EL REFLEJO DE LOS MUROS

Me laceran los muros, los muros, los muros,
todos los muros, los muros propios, los muros ajenos,
la letanía de los muros.

Roberto Manzano
"Poema 18," *Synergos*

THE REFLECTION OF THE WALLS

I am wounded by the walls, the walls, the walls,
all the walls, one's own walls, someone else's walls,
the litany of the walls...

Roberto Manzano
"Poem 18," *Synergos*

LA SILLA DEL PODER

Tuve una silla que daba vueltas como un carrusel.
Sentada miro como se deshacen los papeles inútiles,
aunque inútil es la silla que rota a mi alrededor.
Dar vueltas nos alcanza a subir sobre imágenes abstractas.
Tuve la luz en mis manos para regalar pero no regalé la luz.
Merecerla implica ser buenos con ella en el camino,
implica no subir a la cima con cadáveres en la suela del zapato.
La silla da vueltas como testigo ocular,
como testigo del poder que hace guardar silencio.
Hay quienes odian la luz que sale pura hacia fuera,
buscan tijeras afiladas.
Tuve una silla que daba vueltas,
mientras la probaba sentía el cuerpo desvanecerse.
Dar vueltas nos alcanza a subir entre imágenes abstractas,
nos puede confundir el lugar
incluso,
creernos dueños del polvo que huye del camino.
Apenas pensaba:
un día no habrá sillas que rueden a tu alrededor,
ni siquiera el polvo en ellas para rodarlas nuevamente.
La silla guarda el tiempo,
el cuerpo agujereado por minúsculos espejos,
como quien respira afable a la entrada de un circo.

THE SEAT OF POWER

I had a chair that swiveled like a carousel.
Seated I watch as the worthless papers become a blur,
although useless too is the chair that makes my surroundings spin.
Going in circles allows us to soar over abstract images.
I had the light in my hands to give away but I did not share it.
To be deserving of it means being good along the way,
it means not arriving at the summit with cadavers on the soles of your shoes.
The chair goes in circles like an eyewitness,
like a witness to the power that leads you to keep silent.
There are those who hate the unfiltered light that emanates in the distance,
they search for sharp scissors.
I had a chair that swiveled,
as I tested it I felt my body vanish.
Going in circles allows us to soar over abstract images,
it can even convince us we are somewhere
else,
and make us believe we own the dust we kick up along our journey.
It dawned on me:
One day there will no longer be any chairs to spin you around,
not even dust that kicks up as you spin again and again.
The chair marks time,
the body fragmented by minuscule mirrors,
like one who cheerfully breathes when entering the circus.

EL SALTO DEL PEZ

Ayer fui el pez,
sentí mis escamas a través del tiempo.
Pude mirar con ojos casi de vidrio la distancia,
pude involucrar la paz de todo lo que viene.
Nadie puede remover lo quieto,
las palabras son el sitio permanente,
el salmo de quien las posee.
Pude ser más que el pez.
Mover lo quieto implica el desorden,
el miedo a decir nos desvanece.
Somos el sentido de las cosas sobre el agua.
Ayer fui el pez.

A FISH'S LEAP

Yesterday I was a fish.
I felt my scales across the ages.
I was able to see off into the distance with glass-like eyes.
I was able to find peace in everything to come.
No one can shake what is still.
Words are a permanent place,
the psalm of the one who has them.
I was able to be more than a fish.
To disturb what is still means disorder,
the fear of speaking makes us disappear.
We are the meaning of all things over the water.
Yesterday I was a fish.

EL DESFILE

Desfile es una palabra que tiene que ver con el color rojo. Los colores incitan a caminar sobre el asfalto, así llegamos a entender la abulia en el reflejo de la verdad.

THE PARADE

Parade is a word that is all about the color red. Colors invite us to walk on the asphalt, and thus we come to understand indifference in the face of truth.

AMANECER

Madre de Dios. Desventurados antiguos. Sacrificio infeliz el de los alces que procuran una ceremonia gastada por los siglos. Huir. El ciervo y la flauta de los magos. El niño y la escampada llena de colillas de algún extranjero, de algún duende mágico que suelte monedas al harapo en sombrero fallecido. Cara y niño despacio. Ciervo.

DAYBREAK

Holy Mother. Ancient longsuffering ones. Unfortunate is the sacrifice made by the elk that fulfill a ritual worn by centuries. Flee. The stag and the magician's flute. The child and the clearing littered with cigarette butts from some foreigner, from some enchanted imp, who tosses coins to the tattered under a lifeless hat. Slow child, face. The stag.

LAS COSAS

La realidad es el beneficio de estar en el lugar apropiado y convertir los juegos de sonreír en todas las cosas de la realidad. Sonreír es ser aunque no estés en el lugar apropiado, porque la realidad de las cosas es lo que uno ve día tras día como un sacrificio.

THINGS

Reality is the benefit of being in the right place and changing the game of smiling into everything that is real. Smiling is being, even if you're not in the right place, because the reality of things is what you see day after day as a sacrifice.

EL PAYASO
A ALEXIS GUERRA

Tuve un amigo poeta que trabajaba de payaso en las tardes con su novia. Un día me invitó a un café y terminamos leyendo hasta la noche. Luego lloramos esperando el amanecer porque no tenía a su ciudad guardada en los bolsillos. Tuve un amigo poeta que trabajaba de payaso para una ciudad.

THE CLOWN
TO ALEXIS GUERRA

I had a poet friend who performed as a clown with his girlfriend in the afternoons. One day we went out for a cup of coffee and wound up reading all night. Later on we wept while we waited for the sun to rise because he didn't have his city tucked away in his pockets. I had a poet friend who worked as a clown for a city.

EL POETA

El poeta estaba muerto y dijo: *Aquí estoy escribiendo tu mundo sobre el mío, escribiendo la vida y el mundo juntos, navegando porque todo es andar, y las cosas suelen convertirse en fuego contra tu espalda si dejas de amar con furia los espacios, si dejas de tocar el secreto del ave, el misterio de un amor que no es amor, ni es canto, ni es caricia.* El poeta estaba muerto porque mató a Pessoa. El poeta eran todos que se multiplicaban y dijo: *Aquí estoy regalando el esplendor de la naturaleza porque existe, sobre todo porque se sabe que existe desde su oscuridad, porque sobre los hombros nace el alba.*

THE POET

The poet was dead, and he said: *Here I am penning your world over mine, penning life and the world together, navigating because everything is about the journey, and things have a way of turning into fire against your back if you stop loving spaces furiously, if you cease to understand the secret of birds, the mystery of a love that isn't love, nor is it song, nor is it a caress.* The poet was dead because he had killed Pessoa. The poet was all those who multiply, and he said: *Here I am bestowing you with the splendor of nature because it exists, more than anything else because it is known to exist from its darkness, because upon all shoulders the dawn breaks.*

EL PASEO

Un perro camina los adoquines y me duermo otra vez con los ojos abiertos. Miro a ese perro gris con hambre de perro no verde, porque no tiene en la boca un hueso que lamer. Como yo, que vuelo hacia un portón semiabierto no verde. Una imagen de Ernesto sobre la pared ahuecada me mira. Oigo a Silvio con su río también ahuecado. Somos todos humildes, utópicos, ahuecados. Hay un pájaro amarillo y verde en mi puerta. Siempre me espera con ganas de comer, lo espero con ganas de verlo volar, él me espera en la puerta como esperando a que yo vuele. Camino hacia el portón no verde con los ojos abiertos.

STROLLING

A dog ambles across the cobblestones and I nod off again with my eyes still open. I gaze at that gray dog with his greenless, doggish hunger because his mouth is missing a bone to lick. He's like me, as I glide toward a half-open, greenless gate. A picture of Ernesto on the hollow wall looks back at me. I hear Silvio with his river that is also hollow. We are all humble, utopic, hollow. There is a yellow-green bird in my doorway. He always waits for me eager to eat; I always wait for him, eager to see him fly. He waits for me in the doorway as if waiting for me to fly. I walk toward the greenless gate with eyes still open.

EL CUADRO
A LESTER CAMPA

Hay un cuadro. Allí me desplomo y hablo sola sin temor a que me escuchen. Es bueno saber que nadie te escucha. El pensamiento es como la soledad. No pienso en la muerte como otras veces porque duele pensar en morirse. Mirarme nuevamente en el cuadro donde todos miran la isla que sobresale es un buen lugar para el equilibrio.

THE PAINTING
TO LESTER CAMPA

There is a painting. There I break down, and alone I speak without worrying that someone may hear me. It's good to know no one is listening to you. Thinking is like solitude. I don't think about death as before because it's painful to think about dying. Looking at myself again in the painting while everyone else looks at the conspicuous island, it's a good place to find your balance.

MINUTOS EN EL PARQUE

Las horas corren atravesando los parques. La llovizna
cae deprisa sobre los párpados. Hoy es un día triste.
Guardo la minúscula gota que poseo. Se ha roto la
hojarasca de mi leve sonrisa y vuelve de los muertos la
otra. Mis horas corren atravesando los parques.

MINUTES IN THE PARK

Time runs through the parks. Mist falls heavily upon my eyelids. Today is a sad day. I safeguard a minuscule drop in my hands. The fallen leaf of my thin smile has broken and my other self returns from the dead. My time runs through the parks.

LA DANZA

El parque es mío. Camino descalza por él y apenas siento el dolor, mis pies danzan en su sombra. Es mi parque el tiempo húmedo y el reloj apagado. No me importa si muero bailando sobre él, no me importa si alguien me encierra en su celda por bailar desnuda. El parque es mío.

THE DANCE

The park is mine. I wander barefoot through it scarcely feeling any pain. My feet dance among its shadows. Humid time and an unwound watch are my park. It doesn't matter if I die dancing in it. It doesn't matter if someone locks me up in its cell for dancing naked. The park is mine.

MÁSCARAS

A la puerta de los arrecifes puntiagudos está la ciudad. Yo, sentada en los arrecifes puntiagudos, pensando cómo hacer con esta máscara pensante mientras el polvo se sube a los muebles comiéndoles el brillo. Odio el polvo. Las máscaras pensantes son pocas. A las puertas de los arrecifes puntiagudos está la ciudad. Yo, sentada con la máscara puesta. No hay otra salida. El polvo entra por doquier.

MASKS

At the edge of the jagged reefs lies the city. I, seated on the jagged reefs, wonder what to do with this rational mask while dust collects on the furniture consuming its shine. I hate dust. Rational masks are but few. At the edge of the jagged reefs lies the city. I, seated with my mask on. There's no other way out. Dust comes in everywhere.

LA NADA

No soy protagonista de nada,
ni siquiera personaje de cuentos pasajeros,
pero intento escribir este poema,
placer húmedo en mi memoria,
alcance sólido y frágil en tus manos.
Es un laberinto mi soledad,
el goce plasmado de los días
como semilla incierta.

NOTHINGNESS

I am not the protagonist of anything,
not even a character in a trivial story,
but I strive to write this poem,
a damp pleasure in my mind,
grasped tangibly and frailly in your hands.
A labyrinth is my solitude,
an indulgence sown through the days
like an uncertain seed.

CAÍN

No entiendo a Yahveh:
separemos el sol de la luna,
separemos al hombre de la mujer,
separemos los bienes,
separemos el agua de la tierra,
separemos a los muertos de los vivos,
huyamos de las serpientes.
Al final,
la sangre de Caín está por doquier.

CAIN

I don't understand Yahweh:
Let us separate the sun and the moon,
Let us separate man from woman,
Let us separate our possessions,
Let us separate water from the land,
Let us separate the dead from the living,
Let us flee from the serpents.
In the end,
the blood of Cain is everywhere.

MUROS

Esta ciudad se inclina sobre ti, apenas tiene un pozo navegable. El muro más feliz se irá cayendo. Tus manos lavadas al sol ya son las verdaderas. Percibe los olores, el nacimiento tierno de un ave, la ofrenda de cada tiempo intacto. Al mismo tiempo de los muros volverás a nacer. Ya se inscribe tu furia sobre el lago, el inicio de no ser mariposa, esa niña despierta, esa ropa de niña zurcida por los peces. Nos queda poco tiempo para bailar apenas sobre esta cicatriz. Somos pequeños cuerpos en el aire.

WALLS

The city leans over you. It scarcely has a well that is navigable. The happiest wall will come tumbling down. Your hands bathed in sunlight are now the genuine ones. Soak in the smells, the tender birth of a bird, the offering of time unbroken. In concert with the walls you will be born anew. Your ire is already inscribed upon the lake, the beginning of not being a butterfly, that young girl now awake, that young girl's clothing darned by fish. We have but little time to dance upon this scar. We are small bodies in the air.

EL MAR

No hay tijeras que corten la soga de mi cuello frente al mar, no hay lancha esperando al viejo pescador semidesnudo. Hay soga con nudo alrededor de mi cuello, no tijeras ni lanchas esperando al viejo pescador que sabe. Pudo un hombre cruzar sin soga alrededor de su cuello. Pudo resistir un hombre y cruzar sin soga frente al mar.

THE SEA

Standing before the sea there are no scissors that can cut the noose from my neck. There is no boat waiting for the old half-naked fisherman. There is only a knotted noose about my neck, and neither scissors nor boats waiting for the old fisherman who knows. A man succeeded in crossing over without a noose about his neck. He was able to resist and cross over without a noose before the sea.

SALIENDO DE MÍ

Salgo de mí,
caminando como perdida,
adorando el tiempo que me queda
con el corazón extraño,
casi doloroso y tierno entre la gente.
Salgo de mí,
sé de pronto lo que hay en tu pecho,
lo que aplaude el bufón de mis sentidos.
Me avergüenzo de sentir en este sitio la hojarasca
la alfombra mágica que nos desvela.
Salgo de mí,
sola,
húmeda de amarlo todo,
confundida.

TAKING LEAVE OF MYSELF

I take leave of myself,
walking around as if lost,
worshipping the time that remains
with an uncanny heart,
somewhat painful and tender among the others.
I take leave of myself,
and suddenly I know what's in your heart,
what the jester within my feelings applauds.
I am ashamed of feeling in this place the fallen leaves,
the magic carpet that keeps us awake.
I take leave of myself,
alone,
damp from loving everything,
confused.

DENEGADOS

Viajes, remesas familiares. Eso tiene un nombre apócrifo o narcótico. Pasaporte, seguro de vida, sello de diez pesos convertibles. Agencia DHL si olvidas los papeles necesarios. Fotocopias recientes de las páginas uno y dos, cuños sin discurso del porqué se viaja a otro minuto de vida, perfume y cascarilla debajo del zapato, flores amarillas y azules para cruzar el mar. Cruz en la espalda por si ese día coges el virus de la demencia. Demencia no es viajar sin seguro de vida hacia lo desconocido. Demencia es vivir sin viajar hacia lo desconocido. Viajes, remesas familiares. No se tira la muchacha debajo del camión con papeles que dicen Denegado, se tira en una balsa hecha de corcho y cámaras del camión. Luego aparece su rostro en los arrecifes. Muchacha que sueña con viajes y remesas familiares. Hoy yace con mordiscos de peces salvajes en la bahía.

DENIED

Travels, remittances from relatives. Such an apocryphal or narcotic name. Passport, life insurance, a seal that costs ten pesos in convertible currency. DHL in case you forget any obligatory papers. Recent photocopies of pages one and two, affixed stamps without lengthy explanation as to why you're travelling to another way of life, perfume and magical egg shell powder on the sole of your shoe, yellow and blue flowers for crossing the sea. A cross on your back should you come down with a viral case of dementia. Dementia doesn't mean making the journey without insurance for the unknown. Dementia is living without making the journey towards the unknown. Travels, remittances from relatives. The young girl doesn't throw herself under an oncoming truck with her papers that say "Denied." She throws herself in a raft made of cork and inner tubes. Later on her face appears out on the reefs. A young girl who dreams of travels and remittances from relatives. Today she floats in the bay gnawed by savage fish.

DESNUDOS
A SIGMUND SOBOLIESKI

Hay un lugar con un señor que no habla de abedules, ni
liebres corriendo por la nieve. Con casaca gris y estrella
colgando de sus manos también grises. Dice Auschwitz. Sus
ojos comienzan a quebrarse como el cristal de la noche en
la barraca sin liebre corriendo tranquila por la nieve. Detrás
de la bellota una ardilla se perdió, se ha congelado mirando
Auschwitz, un lugar perdido entre los muertos. Buscan el
reposo al no entender qué hacen en el mismo río, vagando
desnudos. Vistiendo a rayas aún con el número 88 tatuado
en su brazo, exclama: "Todos corrimos hacia la luz. ¿Dónde
estaba Dios?"

NAKED
TO SIGMUND SOBOLIESKI

There is a place with a man who does not speak of birch trees or hares running through the snow. With his gray cassock and star hanging from his gray hands. He utters Auschwitz. His eyes begin to shatter like the night's pane in the barracks without hares running tranquilly through the snow. Behind an acorn a squirrel is lost, frozen as it gazes upon Auschwitz, a place lost among the dead. They long for rest, wandering naked, still not understanding what brings them to this very river. Dressed in stripes with the number 88 tattooed on his arm, he exclaims: "We all ran towards the light. Where was God?"

DESCUBRIRSE

Descubro una flor,
cada día descubro que la flor
no tiene el mismo olor que las otras,
que pronto dejará de ser flor
para quienes la han visto como yo,
sola y desnuda,
sin que nadie antes la mirase.
Descubro el infinito de no ser,
y mientras camino,
me limito a respirar el mismo acento de los hombres.
Dime cómo hacer,
si entonces estos versos no llegan a ningún sitio
donde las flores siempre existieron.

DISCOVERY

I discover a flower,
each day I discover that one flower
doesn't have the same smell as the others,
that soon it will cease to be a flower
for those who have seen it as I,
alone and naked,
without anyone having seen it before.
I discover the infinity of not being,
and while I stroll,
I merely breathe in the common accent of men.
Tell me then what shall I do
if these verses never make it to places
where flowers always existed.

DEL TIEMPO

Hay un día exacto en que todos piensan lo mismo,
una hora exacta en que muere alguien con su mano en el pecho.
Hay un lugar donde se espera una flor,
una guitarra colgando de los hombros,
una casa invisible en la colina.
Hay un día en que todos perdemos la noche
porque nunca la tuvimos,
en que fuimos al viaje más largo a través de la luz.
Hay un lugar de dos que no es de nadie.

ABOUT TIME

There is an exact day when everyone thinks alike,
a precise moment when someone dies with a hand on their heart.
There is a place where a flower is expected,
a guitar slung over one's shoulders,
an invisible house on the hill.
There is a day when all of us lose the night
because we never had it,
when we set out through the light on the ultimate voyage.
There is a place for two that belongs to no one.

LA AVENIDA

Anduve despacio por la avenida,
Era el sonido quien servía la paz en el viento,
era mi sombra y yo caminando,
como extrañadas por el remolino de las hojas
que no son más que hadas improvisando la tarde.
El árbol espera callado,
nadie sostiene sus ramas como un velo necesario.
Anduve despacio por la avenida,
los gatos miraban queriendo adivinar el pensamiento,
miraban con ojos de animal silencioso.
Nadie esconde un cuerpo en la penumbra.
En la avenida dos muchachos se abrazan.
Temen que las brujas fatídicas de Macbeth
cambien el rumbo de las cosas.

THE AVENUE

I sauntered along the avenue.
It was the sound that created peace in the wind,
it was my shadow and I walking,
as if lost in a whirlwind of leaves
that are nothing more than faeries improvising the afternoon.
The tree waits silently,
no one holds up its branches as a necessary veil.
I sauntered along the avenue,
the cats gazed back trying to guess my thoughts,
they stared with the eyes of a silent animal.
No one hides a body in the shadows.
On the street two young men embrace each other.
They fear Macbeth's fatidic witches
may change the course of events.

ORACIÓN CONTRA EL SUEÑO

¿Será que siempre buscas una alfombra? ¿Que no estaremos sentados donde mismo y la gente nos pisoteará desnudos, cabizbajos a la semilla de ser alguien? ¿Será que no tendremos unicornios porque estarán perdidos? ¿Será que todo está encima de mí y debo aplastarlos para descubrir *al tonto de la colina*, o será que nunca fuimos?

A PRAYER TO CAST AWAY DREAMS

Is it possible that you'll keep on looking for a flying carpet, that we won't be seated where we are right now, that people won't be stepping on us while we're naked, with our head down on the verge of becoming someone? Is it feasible there'll no longer be unicorns because they've gone astray? Could it be that everything hovers over me and I must squelch all of it if I am to find the fool on the hill, or is it that we never were?

EL OLVIDO

Estamos solos en la arena desprovista de arcángeles, adorando intranquilos el amanecer. Solos y ciegos. Atravesando los síntomas febriles de la distancia dentro del circo. Quisiera quitar las manchas en mi blusa. No estamos solos. Estamos condenados a lo que ya pasó.

OBLIVION

We are alone in the sand void of archangels, worshipping restlessly the sunrise. Alone and blind. Passing through feverish symptoms of the distance within the circus. If I could only remove the stains from my blouse. We are not alone. We are condemned to live the past.

SIRGADORES

Corren los paramédicos. País es la clave o arrecifes mirando hacia los traficantes de hombres que se alejan. País es la clave de toda una mercancía barata. Fuego contra la naciente luz. El barquero escupe su cigarro mordido con el temor de hundirse hacia el hueco de todos los ángeles. Los sirgadores alguna vez tuvieron una isla. Corren los paramédicos como una mentira hacia el fondo. Ya no están cubiertos de santos ni botellas de agua como las que cuelgan hoy en un museo de Liverpool. Fuego contra la naciente luz que sale y se aleja.

THE DECKHANDS

The paramedics scamper. The nation is the key, reefs that watch the human traffickers sail away. The nation is the key for a whole pack of cheap merchandise. Fire against the nascent light. The captain spits his chawed cigar anxious that he might sink into the angel's abyss. Once upon a time the deckhands had their own island. The paramedics rush into the background like a lie. No longer are they covered with saints and water bottles like the ones now displayed in a museum in Liverpool. Fire against the nascent light that flares up and fades away.

DE LOS TECHOS
A JUAN C. VALLS

Estás lejos,
dejando las ciudades vacías,
los muchachos desnudos por la lluvia.
Todo queda aislado como una multitud de hombres,
como una noticia,
la de no estar entre los que te anuncian.
A esta hora debes estar cansado de estrellarte con tus guerreros,
de ser siempre el que inicia los sitios.
Estar feliz no es para los que buscan estar felices,
es para el que no sabe nada de amores.

FROM THE ROOFTOPS
TO JUAN C. VALLS

You're far away,
having left behind empty cities,
young ones stripped by the rain.
Everything remains apart like a mob of men,
as if it were news,
news that you are not present among those who announce you.
By now you must be tired of clashing with your warriors,
tired of always being the one to initiate the sieges.
Being happy doesn't come to those who seek to be happy.
It comes to the one who knows nothing of love.

...SOLO ES MÍA LA PURA SOLEDAD
A DULCE MARÍA LOYNAZ

Eres losa intranquila,
mármol blanco brillando sobre el agua,
cuencas de vidrio en lámparas rompientes.
El viento tras los árboles aplaca los sentidos,
barren el polvo de los muebles tan silenciosamente acomodados.
¿Quién eres que te apagas y vuelves encendida,
con tu elegante paso de amapola silvestre?
¿Quién alza sobre ti la corona de aves como esta soledad?
Tus inquilinos vuelven de sus tumbas,
convierten tu fantasma en aire y luz,
en madera preciosa sosteniendo entre piedras el águila.
¿Cómo eres tan hábil circundándolo todo,
rastro comediante de tu jardín?
Esta casa es tu isla innegociable,
tu sombra se ha escondido de Cupido,
la veo asomarse discreta tras las cortinas.
Tu flor no ha marchitado debajo de la almohada.

...PURE SOLITUDE IS MINE ALONE
TO DULCE MARÍA LOYNAZ

You are a restless tile,
white marble that glistens on the water,
glass beads on shattering chandeliers.
The breeze through the trees soothes my senses,
it sweeps the dust away from the furniture so silently situated.
Who might you be that you shroud yourself and return illuminated
with your elegant gait of wild poppies?
Who if not solitude could coronate you with this crown of birds?
Your tenants return from their tombs,
they turn your specter into air and light,
into precious hardwood that bears the eagle among stones.
How are you so capable of encompassing it all,
even a playful trace from your garden?
This dwelling is your unnegotiable island,
your shadow has concealed itself from Cupid,
I see it discreetly spy from behind the curtains.
Your flower has not withered beneath your pillow.

INSOMNIO

No duermo. Unas personas rompen los cristales de una fábrica a la salida del estadio. La ira los confunde. Son las monedas y el peso de la isla. Es el deseo repentino de viajar. Escapé de tus manos como un ave que emigra hacia el invierno. No rompo cristales en la noche, vuelvo a tu ausencia desnuda.

RESTLESSNESS

I can't sleep. Some people are breaking the windowpanes of a factory as they come from the stadium. They are confused by rage. It is the currency and the burden of the Island. It is the sudden urge to travel. I slipped through your hands like a bird flying south for the winter. I don't shatter windowpanes at night. I head back to your bare absence.

EL ÁNGEL

Hay un puente semejante a una hormiga por donde pasan todos los enanos transparentes. Saltan a la cúspide cuando ven al ángel humedecer sus alas en el lago. Hay un puente, todos se lavan la cara con sus alas. A mitad del paseo en el bosque llora un ángel.

THE ANGEL

Reminiscent of an ant, there is a bridge where diaphanous dwarfs happen by. Whenever they see the angel dipping its wings in the lake they spring to the summit. There is a bridge, and all use his wings to wash their face. Halfway along the forest trail an angel cries.

PESCADORES

Cerca de un puente frente al mar hay una casa grande a medio construir. Siempre quise vivir frente al mar. La miro en el vacío. Los pescadores suben a la isla todos los peces rosados. Miro decepcionada la imagen del pescador que sube los peces a la isla. Cerca de un puente frente al mar hay un vendedor de peces rosados. Pienso que debieron esconderse en la primavera. Ya no quiero ser el pez.

FISHERMEN

Near a bridge facing the sea, there is a big house half-finished. I always wanted to live across from the ocean. I gaze at it in all its vastness. The fishermen bring back to the Island their loads of pink fish. Disheartened I am struck by the image of a fisherman hoisting his fish upon the Island. Near a bridge facing the sea, there is a man selling pink fish. I think they should have shrouded themselves in the spring. I no longer wish to be a fish.

VOLVER

Vuelvo a tu piel desnuda,
cruzo un puente,
viajo,
voy recogiendo los silencios,
parto hacia el viento,
no me ves,
vuelvo a tu piel desnuda.

COMING BACK

I come back to your bare skin,
I cross a bridge,
I meander,
I go along collecting silences,
I set off for the wind,
You don't notice me,
I come back to your bare skin.

HAY UN PUEBLO QUE INCITA
A CAMINAR DESNUDOS

Hay un pueblo que incita a caminar desnudos,
a mirarse en sus aguas casi muertas de miedo
por el escombro que a veces seduce.
Un pueblo está en la mano de una iglesia,
tocan la filarmónica como cantándole a los que se evaporan,
a los que huyen como garzas en busca de aguas limpias,
de insectos que no estén contaminados.
Hoy los parques se embriagan con cerveza,
sustituyen el té por alcohol,
las vírgenes huyen al techo sin campanas.
Tengo un pueblo pequeño
metido entre la tráquea y el corazón,
sus puentes están fríos
como si de pronto alguien soñara con la nieve.
¿A dónde fueron a parar las aguas de la fuente?,
¿los mangles felices de Quidiello?,
¿Silvio con su guitarra de madera en los montes?,
¿dónde Alexander fotografiando muros?
Su amor a los aviones lo alejó del ocaso,
de la mirada pura hacia el Abela,
hacia El Loco que atrae a los turistas.
Sus fotos quedaron,
como el musgo que se come mi tortuga cuando no tiene el pan.
Hay un pueblo que incita a caminar desnudos
y yo quiero pasearlo de tu mano.

THERE'S A TOWN THAT TEMPTS YOU TO WALK AROUND NAKED

There's a town that tempts you to walk around naked,
to look at yourself in its waters almost dead with fear
from the ruins that too often seduce us.
A town lies in the hand of a church.
They play the harmonica as if singing for those who evaporate,
for those who flee like herons in search of clean waters,
in search of insects that aren't diseased.
Today its parks get drunk on beer,
they substitute tea with alcohol,
its virgins bolt to the bell-less rooftops.
I have a small town
stuck between my trachea and heart.
Its bridges are frozen over
as if suddenly someone had dreamed about snow.
Where have the waters of its fountains come to rest?
The cheerful mangroves in Quidiello's paintings?
Silvio with his wooden guitar out in the forest?
Where is Alexander photographing the walls?
His love for planes took him away from the sunset,
from his pure vision of Abela's work,
of El Loco who charms the tourists.
His photos remained behind,
like the moss that my turtle eats when there's nothing more to feed it.
There's a town that tempts you to walk around naked
and I want to share it with you hand in hand.

SEPTIEMBRE

Esa noche esperaba,
pensaba sobre mi imán,
sobre el polvo excluido de las calles.
Anduve desnuda por el corredor
hasta sentir el frío sobre mi piel cayendo,
atravesé muy lenta los olores de mi hija y su perro,
esperé a mi amor como todos los días de septiembre.
Supe de pronto amarga la noticia que circundó mi espacio,
esperé paciente la hojarasca sobre mi espina,
retiré mis armas bajo tierra,
recordé un paseo de Alfonsina por su jardín.
Morí,
no quedé a salvo del horror,
morí como el nenúfar sobre el río delicado.
Esa mañana no quise tomar café,
esperaba a mi amor como todos los días de septiembre.

SEPTEMBER

That particular night I was waiting,
thinking about my magnet,
about the dirt shut out from the streets.
I walked around the hall naked
until I felt the cold fall upon my skin,
I slowly passed through the smells of my daughter and her dog,
I waited for my love like every day in September.
Suddenly I realized the bitter truth that invaded my space,
I patiently endured the leaf storm that ran up and down my spine,
below the earth I drew in my arms,
I remembered a stroll that Alfonsina took around her garden.
I died,
I wasn't safe from the horror,
I died as the water lily upon the delicate river.
That morning I didn't want to have a cup of coffee,
I waited for my love like every day in September.

TRANSPARENCIA

Un ave puede ser lo más hermoso que atraviesa la carpa. Me dirás que siempre llevas el alma como lanzándote cada invierno, que existe una luz en el mar algo distraída, y recogerás el cuerpo manchado por no ser la tarde. Estar sola es como caminar en un cuarto oscuro sin más juguete que la gloria del pez.

TRANSPARENCY

A bird can be the most beautiful thing to pass over the tent. You will probably tell me that you always bear your soul as if hurling yourself each winter, that there is a light a bit distracted in the sea, and you will gather up your body stained because it's not the afternoon. To be alone is like walking in a dark room without any toy other than the glory of the fish.

EL AFILADOR DE TIJERAS

El afilador de tijeras pregona. Un muchacho dejó su perfume de Londres en una de las sillas. Era tierno y callado, apenas transparente. Su cabello era gris como sus ojos. Me mira como quien desnuda un cuerpo para siempre y su idioma confunde mis migajas. Lo acepto y sonrío esquivando el dolor. El afilador de tijeras me mira.

THE SCISSORS SHARPENER

The man who sharpens scissors calls out. A boy left
behind the scent of his London cologne in one of the
chairs. He was sweet and reserved, barely transparent.
His hair was gray as were his eyes. He stares at me as
if he were undressing a body forever and his language
misreads my crumbs. I accept it and smile dodging
the pain. The scissors sharpener looks at me.

EL SITIO DE LOS SALMOS
A LISANDRA

Eres la odisea ventajosa de la lluvia, tal vez inalcanzable por la furia de los peces, por el mar terrible que hay entre dos islas. Vuelve sobre mí la otra imagen perversa, la del poeta amaestrado en el sitio de los salmos. Tiemblo sobre mi espalda porque las voces se vuelven minúsculas y yace sobre el tramo de los días. Eres casi siempre la neblina vagando a tientas, desnuda, casi blanca y violenta, casi niña. Soporto el despertar sin tus ojos, la sombra amigable que pasea confiada hacia el puerto, soporto el aguacero en mis piernas cuando vuelas como yo, mitigando inconclusa la canción prohibida. Eres casi siempre mi miedo, el temor de sentir el vacío que engendra la verdad. Soy el sitio de los salmos en la puerta.

THE SITE OF PSALMS
TO LISANDRA

You are the beneficial odyssey of the rain, perhaps inaccessible due to the fury of the fish, due to the terrible sea that surrounds the islands. That other depraved image comes over me, the one of the poet trained in the site of Psalms. My spine shivers because the voices become minuscule and rest upon the measure of days. You are almost always the fog that wanders groping, naked, off-white and violent, almost a child. I endure waking up without your eyes, the friendly shadow that strolls assuredly towards the port. I endure the downpour on my legs when you take off as I do, toning down inconclusively the prohibited song. You are almost always my fear, the fright of feeling the emptiness that truth engenders. I am the site of Psalms at the door.

LOS SILENCIOS

Se sabe que los muros están grises, que las paredes brotan hacia dentro una y otra vez al canto de mi útero. No tenemos que ser los que navegan a alguna parte. Solo el salmo, los sitios esperados. La lluvia palpa mi mano y se hunde en la arena con otras. Soy de este costado que me hinca. Temo la sorpresa de la ciudad. Entierro mi útero y vuelvo a caer en la palma de mi mano, hundida en la arena como siempre.

SILENCES

Everyone knows that the walls are gray, that time and again they bud inwardly to the pulse of my womb. We do not have to be one of those who journey to other parts. Only the psalm, the expected places. The rain caresses my hand and it sinks down into the sand with the others. I belong to this side that jabs at me. I fear the surprise of my city. I bury my womb and I collapse once again in the palm of my hand, sunken in the sand like always.

ANOCHECER

Caminamos sin prisa por la ciudad vacía,
desnuda y descubierta.
Somos la sombra que transcurre entre adoquines,
extranjeros sin prisa.
Padre nuestro,
te pido perdón por la mentira de la nieve,
por su trampa fugaz como mordida.
Venga a nosotros tu reino
y no nos abandones en la ausencia del hombre
que es la bestia.
Perdona su furia como nosotros perdonamos.
Somos corderos del vacío hacia la luz,
eternos confundidos de la sagrada infancia,
pensadores del sexo,
conocidos.
No nos dejes caer en la tentación
y líbranos, señor, cuando la claridad nos oscurece.
Amén.

NIGHTFALL

We saunter through the empty city,
it is naked and exposed.
We are the shadow that stretches across the cobblestones,
unhurried foreigners.
Our Father,
forgive me for lying about the snow,
for its fleeting lure that gnashes.
May your kingdom come
and abandon us not in the absence of man
who is really the beast.
Forgive him his fury as we too forgive.
We are lambs of the emptiness that look to the light,
everlastingly confused about the holy infancy,
fixated on the carnal,
mere acquaintances.
Lead us not into temptation
and free us, O Lord, when clarity overshadows us.
Amen.

LA OVEJA NEGRA

Negra es una oveja que hay en las familias. La oveja negra de mi familia no espera un porvenir brillante. No aprende la lección sobre símbolos patrios, ni supera su miedo a caer. La oveja negra de mi familia se esconde en los techos y mira la noche que no aguarda tampoco el porvenir. La oveja negra nunca es igual que las demás ovejas. Sueña la verdad que no existe, de cómo cruzar tranquila los pueblos de otros lugares y mirar la noche desde los techos. La familia de la oveja negra no enseña cómo soportar la realidad que consume sus hilos diariamente. Sus hilos y su carne cubren los cuerpos desnudos del invierno y dan alegría a otros seres que no miran la noche desde los techos.

BLACK SHEEP

Families have their black sheep. The future for the one in mine is not too promising. She hasn't learned her lessons about patriotic symbols nor has she overcome her fear of falling. The black sheep in my family hides on the rooftops and gazes out upon the night that also doubts the future. The black sheep is never the same as the other sheep. She dreams about a truth that doesn't exist, about strolling casually through towns in other places, about contemplating the night from the roof. The black sheep's family does not try to teach her how to tolerate the reality that daily consumes its own fibers. Its fibers and flesh cover winter's exposed bodies and bring happiness to the others who do not look out at the night from the rooftops.

SOBRE LA AUTORA

Zurelys López Amaya (La Habana, 1967). Poeta, narradora y periodista. Licenciada en Comunicación Social, Universidad de La Habana. Su obra ha sido publicada dentro y fuera de la isla; poesía, entrevistas y reseñas literarias de su autoría se han incluido en revistas nacionales e internacionales. Entre los libros publicados se encuentra el poemario *Pactos con la sombra* (Ediciones Unicornio, 2009); *Rebaños* (Ediciones Extramuros, 2010)—(ambos con re-edición por la Editorial Atom Press, Florida EU, 2010); *Minúsculos espejos* (Editorial Latin Heritage Foundation, Washington, D.C., 2011); *La señora solitaria* (Ediciones Unión, 2013); *Lanzar la Piedra,* con la escritora española Verónica Aranda (Ediciones Corazón de Mango, Colombia, 2015); *Levitaciones* (Ediciones Matanzas, 2015); y *La vela y el náufrago (Editorial Polibea, España, 2016).* Es Miembro de la UNEAC (Unión Nacional de Escritores y Artistas de Cuba). Actualmente trabaja como especialista del Centro de Información de Escritores sobre Literatura Cubana Contemporánea en el Centro Cultural Dulce María Loynaz en La Habana.

ABOUT THE AUTHOR

Zurelys López Amaya (La Habana, 1967). Poet, writer of fiction, and journalist. López Amaya is a graduate of the University of Havana in Communications. Her work has been published both on the island and off; her poems, interviews and literary reviews have been included in diverse national and international journals and magazines. Among her published works are the poetry collections: *Pactos con la sombra* (Unicornio Press, 2009) and *Rebaños* (Extramuros Press, 2010)—both also reedited by Atom Press in Florida in 2010; *Minúsculos espejos* (Latin Heritage Foundation, Washington D.C., 2011); *La señora solitaria* (Unión, 2013); *Lanzar la Piedra,* with Spanish writer Verónica Aranda (Corazón de Mango, Colombia, 2015); *Levitaciones* (Matanzas, Havana, 2015); and *La vela y el náufrago* (Editorial Polibea, Spain, 2016). She is a member of the National Syndicate of Cuban Writers and Artists (UNEAC). Currently she works as a specialist in the Center for Information on Contemporary Cuban Literary Writers at the Dulce María Loynaz Cultural Center in Havana.

SOBRE EL TRADUCTOR

Jeffrey C. Barnett es Profesor de Lenguas Románicas y sirve como Director del Programa de Estudios Latinoamericanos y Caribeños en la Universidad de Washington y Lee (Lexington, Virginia). Ha vivido en Honduras, México y España. Desde 1989 ha enseñado cursos en los campos de lengua, cultura y literatura tanto en su propia universidad como en el extranjero, incluso cursos sobre la novela hispanoamericana del Boom, literatura caribeña, y traducción literaria. Sus estudios sobre la narrativa hispanoamericana y estudios sobre literatura comparativa han aparecido en revistas en España, Latinoamérica, y EEUU. Ha traducido una variedad de autores latinoamericanos. Entre los más recientes figuran *The Memory of Silence / Memoria del silencio* (Cubanabooks, 2014) por Uva de Aragón y "Litany of an Orchid" / "Letanía de una orquídea" por Carlos Fuentes (*Exchanges*, 2015). Su traducción de *Rebaños / Flocks* se destaca como su primera traducción de un volumen de poesía. Cuando no se encuentra en la aula universitaria ni en sus esfuerzos de traducción, pasa el tiempo en largos recorridos en su moto para encontrar inspiración para su blog, *"From the Road: The Moto-Odysseys of the Big Papi."*

ABOUT THE TRANSLATOR

Jeffrey C. Barnett is Professor of Romance Languages and serves as the Latin American and Caribbean Studies Program Head at Washington and Lee University (Lexington, Virginia). He has lived in Honduras, Mexico, and Spain. Since 1989 he has taught classes on language, culture, and literature both domestically and abroad, including courses on the Spanish-American Boom novel, Caribbean literature, and literary translation. His articles on Spanish-American narrative and comparative literary studies have appeared in journals in Spain, Latin America, and the U.S. He has translated a diverse selection of Latin American authors, most recently Uva de Aragón's *The Memory of Silence / Memoria del silencio* (Cubanabooks, 2014) and Carlos Fuentes' "Litany of an Orchid" / "Letanía de una orquídea" (*Exchanges,* 2015). His translation of Zurelys Lopez Amaya's *Rebaños / Flocks* marks his first book-length translation of a poetic work. When not in the classroom or translating, he spends his time riding cross country on his motorcycle to find inspiration for his blog, *"From the Road: The Moto-Odysseys of the Big Papi."*

ALSO AVAILABLE FROM CUBANABOOKS
OTROS TÍTULOS DE CUBANABOOKS

Always Rebellious/Cimarroneando
Poems by Georgina Herrera/coordinated by Juanamaría
Cordones-Cook
ISBN 978-0-9827860-6-2
INTERNATIONAL LATINO BOOK AWARD WINNER!
Poetry of origin, pain, heartbreak, and consolation by Afro-
Cuban Georgina Herrera.

An Address in Havana/Domicilio habanero
Short stories by María Elena Llana/translated by Barbara Riess
ISBN 978-0-9827860-3-1
INTERNATIONAL LATINO BOOK AWARD WINNER!
Solitary characters, afflicted by real or fictitious fears…a world
plagued with absurdities…. Exceptional stories, told through
a subjectively ironic perspective with both humor and an
evenhanded cruelty.

Disconnect/Desencuentro
Short stories by Nancy Alonso/translated by Anne Fountain
ISBN 978-0-9827860-1-7
Irony and subtle humor permeate these stories that explore
sexuality, morality, and coincidence in present-day Cuba.

Havana Is a Really Big City/La Habana es una ciudad bien grande
Short stories by Mirta Yáñez/translated by Sara Cooper, et. al.
ISBN 978-0-9827860-0-0
These humorous and poignant stories that illustrate everyday life
in contemporary Havana will challenge the reader's assumptions
about the Cuban reality.

159

Homing Instincts/Querencias
Poems by Nancy Morejón/translated by Pamela Carmell
ISBN 978-0-9827860-5-5
INTERNATIONAL LATINO BOOK AWARD WINNER!
In this bilingual collection of poetry, Afro-Cuban *belle des letres* Nancy Morejón reveals depths of passion and pride.

Ophelias/Ofelias
Short stories by Aida Bahr/translated by Dick Cluster
ISBN 978-0-9827860-2-4
Ophelias is about eight women pushed to the edge of madness. Their stories could happen anywhere—and they could only happen in Cuba.

The Bleeding Wound/Sangra por la herida
By Mirta Yáñez/translated by Sara E. Cooper
ISBN 978-0-9827860-7-9
INTERNATIONAL LATINO BOOK AWARD WINNER!
A novel of postmodern transcendence and a painful recuperation of memory, with dark humor and irreverence, *The Bleeding Wound* reveals the reality of Cuba—in the heyday of the Revolution and today.

The Memory of Silence/Memoria del silencio
A novel by Uva De Aragón/translated By Jeffrey C. Barnett
ISBN 978-0-9827860-4-8
INTERNATIONAL LATINO BOOK AWARD WINNER!
A metaphor of a nation and its Diaspora, *The Memory of Silence/ Memoria del silencio* transcends the Cuban reality and becomes a story of universal breadth, a triumph of love and family over distance and politics.

160

FORTHCOMING TITLES FROM CUBANABOOKS
FUTUROS TÍTULOS DE CUBANABOOKS

About Spirits & Other Mysteries/Sobre espíritus & otros misterios
Shorts tales by Esther Díaz Llanillo/translation by Manuel Martínez
ISBN 978-1-944176-10-5
The unexpected creeps or lunges into daily life in these quirky stories, in which the characters must struggle against a variety of foes—from ghosts, to inimical forces, to their own fatal flaws.

Gelsomina in the White Madhouse/Desde los blancos manicomios
A novel by Margarita Mateo Palmer/translation by Rebecca Hanssens-Reed
ISBN 978-1-944176-09-9
In this cathartic novel inspired by the author's own battle with the angels and demons of insanity, the main character is a female Don Quijote navigating the confusing and complex reality of post-Soviet Cuba.

The Visits and Other Poems/Las visitas y otros poemas
By Mirta Yáñez/translation by Elizabeth Gamble Miller
ISBN 978-1-944176-11-2
The Visits constitutes a vibrant young poet's spiritual journey through Havana, where Time is given to us, not as a concept but as a vital and flowing experience.

Universo and the List/Universo y la lista
Short stories by Laidi Fernández de Juan/
translation by Mary G. Berg
ISBN 978-1-944176-12-9
Does trafficking in red beans, peas and coffee constitute a serious crime? Interconnected stories explore this and other absurd questions of everyday Cuban life, revealing the seriously humorous perspective of regular Cuban people.

2016 INTERNATIONAL LATINO BOOK AWARDS WINNERS

Best Fiction Book Translation—Spanish to English:

1st Place: *An Address in Havana/Domicilio habanero* by María Elena Llana and translated by Barbara Riess

2nd Place: *The Bleeding Wound/Sangra por la herida* by Mirta Yáñez and translated by Sara E. Cooper

Best Poetry Book—Bilingual:

1st Place: *Always Rebellious/Cimarroneando* by Georgina Herrera and translated by Juanamaría Cordones-Cook

Honorable Mention: *Homing Instincts/Querencias* by Nancy Morejón and translated by Pamela Carmell

Best Novel—Historical Fiction—Bilingual or Spanish:

2nd Place: *The Memory of Silence/Memoria del silencio* by Uva de Aragón and translated by Jeffrey C. Barnett

Cubanabooks

ORDER CUBANANBOOKS TITLES

Distributed by Small Press Distribution
Available through Ingram, Baker & Taylor, and Project Muse
Get paperbacks and e-books on Amazon
Receive discounted prices at www.csuchico.edu/Cubanabooks